Uniquely Illinois

Andrew Santella
AR B.L.: 6.1
Points: 1.0

Uniquely
Illinois

Andrew Santella

Heinemann Library
Chicago, Illinois

© 2003 Reed Educational & Professional Publishing
Published by Heinemann Library,
an imprint of Reed Educational & Professional
Publishing, Chicago, Illinois

Customer Service 888-454-2279

Visit our website at www.heinemannlibrary.com

Designed by Heinemann Library
Page layout by Depke Design
Printed and bound in the United States by Lake
Book Manufacturing, Inc.

07 06 05 04 03
10 9 8 7 6 5 4 3 2 1

**Library of Congress
Cataloging-in-Publication Data**
Santella, Andrew.
  Uniquely Illinois / by Andrew Santella.
     v. cm. -- (State studies)
Includes bibliographical references (p.47) and
index.
Contents: One of a kind -- State government --
Capitals and capitols --
Illinois state symbols -- Land of Lincoln -- World's
fairs -- Illinois's first city -- The Water Tower --
Illinois weather -- Food -- Illinois stores --
Architecture and more -- Parks and more -- Great
books -- Jazz, blues, and more -- Sports -- Even
more unique.
  ISBN 1-40340-012-1 (HC), 1-40340-573-5 (Pbk)
1. Illinois--Juvenile literature. [1. Illinois.] I. Title.
II. State studies (Heinemann Library (Firm))
  F541.3 .S28 2002
  977.3--dc21
                              2002000800

Acknowledgments
The author and publishers are grateful to the
following for permission to reproduce copyright
material:

Cover photographs by (TL-TR): Robert Lifson/
Heinemann Library; Michael Henderson/
Burpee Museum of Natural History; Joseph Sohm,
Visions of America/Corbis; Robert Lifson/
Heinemann Library; (bottom) Bill Ross/Corbis

p. 4T, 7, 23T, 26B, 28, 38L, 40T, 44L AP/Wide World Photos;
p. 4 Cahokia Mounds State Historic Site; pp5, 33
maps.com/Heinemann Library; p. 5T Chicago
Historical Society; p. 5B Mitchell Gerber/Corbis; p. 6 Illinois
Information Service; p. 9 Courtesy Supreme Court of Illinois;
p. 10 David Blanchette, Illinois Historic Preservation Agency;
p. 11T Architect of the Capitol; pp. 11B, 20, 25T, 29T, 30,
34, 39B, 40 Robert Lifson/Heinemann Library; pp. 12, 17B
James P. Rowan; p. 13T Richard Thom/Visuals Unlimited;
p. 13B Jeremy Woodhouse/PhotoDisc; p. 14T Mark A.
Schneider/Photo Researchers; p. 14B Richard Day/Daybreak
Photography; p. 15T Phil Degginger/Animals Animals p. 15B
Stephen J. Kraseman/Photo Researchers; p. 16T Courtesy
Illinois State Museum; p. 16B Graham Bartram/Flag Institute;
p. 17T David R. Frazier; p. 18 Courtesy Illinois Secretary of
State; p. 19 Summy-Birchard, Co./Illinois State Historical
Library; p. 21T Courtesy Illinois Department of Commerce
and Community Affairs; p. 21B Courtesy Lincoln/Logan
County Chamber of Commerce; p. 22 Corbis; p. 23 Illinois
State Historical Library; p. 23B Robert Lifson; p. 24
Community Life at Cahokia by Michael Hampshire/Cahokia
Mounds State Historic Site; p. 25B Courtesy Michael
Gassmann/Downtown Collinsville, Inc.; p. 26T AFP/Corbis;
p. 27 Heinemann Library; pp. 28T, 35, 37 The Granger
Collection, NY; p. 28B 1898 cover: Reprinted by permission
of Sears, Roebuck and Co. Protected by copyright. No
duplication permitted; p. 29 Courtesy Walgreen's; p. 29B
Angelo Hornak/Corbis; p. 31T Courtesy Skidmore, Owings
and Merrill; p. 31B "The Sphinx" 2002 Estate of Pablo
Picasso/Artists Rights Society (ARS), New York; p. 32 Marge
Beaver/Photography Plus; pp. 36B, 40, 42B Bettmann/
Corbis; p. 37 Getty Images; p. 38R Robert Lifson, reproduced
with permission of the Chicago Bulls; p. 39T Claes Oldenburg
and Coosje van Bruggen. Batcolumn, 1977/Steel and
aluminum painted with polyurethane enamel/96 ft. 8 in.
(29.46m) high x 9 ft. 9 in. (2.97 m diameter, on base 4 ft.
(1.22 m) high x 10 ft. (3.05 m diameter/Harold Washington
Social Security Center, 600 West Madison Street, Chicago/
Photo by Attillio Maranzano; p. 39BR Reuters Newmedia
Inc./Corbis; p. 41 Chicago Daily News/ Chicago Historical
Society (#ICHi-23144); p. 42T Courtesy Chicago Bears; p. 42
Brent Jones p. 43 Tom Hauck/Getty Images/Allsport; p. 44R
Hedrich-Blessing and the First United Methodist Church,
Chicago; p. 45 Andrew E. Cook

Special thanks to Tom Schwartz of the Illinois
Historic Preservation Agency, for his expert help and
advice on the series.

Every effort has been made to contact copyright
holders of any material reproduced in this book. Any
omissions will be rectified in subsequent
printings if notice is given to the publisher.

Some words are shown in bold, **like this.**
You can find out what they mean by looking
in the glossary.

Contents

One of a Kind

There is no place quite like Illinois. Only in Illinois can you find the ancient Native American city of Cahokia and the busy modern city of Chicago. Only Illinois is the home of the Sears Tower, one of the world's tallest buildings. It was also the home state of Robert P. Wadlow, the tallest person to ever live.

The first Ferris wheel was part of the 1893 World's Fair in Chicago. Each of its cars held 60 people!

Only in Illinois can you find a river that runs backward, like the Chicago River. And only Illinois can claim to be the birthplace of **skyscrapers,** the Ferris wheel, and the worldwide chain of McDonald's restaurants.

Monks Mound (below) was part of ancient Cahokia. It is the largest prehistoric earthwork in the United States. Visitors can still climb the mound today.

Most importantly, consider the people of Illinois. The Prairie State can claim Abraham Lincoln, Michael Jordan, Jane Addams,

Illinois

Galena • Rockford • Waukegan
Byron • Arlington Heights
Des Plaines
Elgin • Evanston
Dixon • Wheaton • Skokie
Oak Park
Aurora • Chicago
Rock Island • Tampico Naperville
Moline La Salle Joliet
Bishop Hill Kankakee
Galesburg
Peoria • Eureka
Pekin
Nauvoo Bloomington Normal
Champaign Danville
Quincy Urbana
New Salem Springfield Arthur
Lake
Shelbyville Mattoon
Effingham
Godfrey Vandalia
Alton
Edwardsville Carlyle
Lake
East St. Louis
Cahokia Centralia
Mt. Vernon Grayville
Prairie du Rend
Rocher Lake
Kaskaskia
Shawneetown
Carbondale
Cairo

Mississippi River, Rock River, Fox River, Illinois & Michigan Canal, Kankakee River, Illinois River, Sangamon River, Koskaskia River, Embarras River, Wabash River, Big Muddy River, Ohio River

N W E S

0 ____ 50 mi.
0 ____ 50 km

Oprah Winfrey is one of Illinois's most famous residents.

Frank Lloyd Wright, Ernest Hemingway, Oprah Winfrey, Benny Goodman, and many others. Each has called Illinois home, and each has made his or her unique mark on the world. That's the Illinois way. That's what makes Illinois a place unlike any other.

Government

Like the federal government, Illinois's state government is divided into three branches: **executive, legislative,** and **judicial.**

EXECUTIVE

The chief executive of Illinois is the **governor.** He or she is elected by voters and serves a four-year term. The governor is similar to the president of the United States, but on a state level. Each year, the governor submits a **budget** to **lawmakers** for approval. He or she also reviews all new **legislation** proposed by lawmakers. The governor can choose to approve the legislation and make it state law. Or the governor can reject, or **veto,** the legislation.

Other executive officials are the **lieutenant governor, secretary of state, attorney general, treasurer,** and **comptroller.** Like the governor, these officials are elected by voters and serve four-year terms. The lieutenant governor assists the governor. The

The governor's mansion (below) in Springfield is the home of the state's chief executive. It has served as the governor's home since 1855.

secretary of state is responsible for keeping the state's records. He or she issues drivers' licenses and license plates. The attorney general is the chief law enforcement officer of the state. He or she leads efforts to fight crime. The treasurer manages the state's money and decides how it will be **invested.** The comptroller is the chief financial officer of Illinois. He or she writes the checks to pay the state's bills and keeps track of the money spent.

LEGISLATIVE

The state legislature of Illinois is called the General Assembly. It makes state laws. The General Assembly is divided into the state senate and the house of representatives. This is similar to the United States Congress, but on a state level. There are 59 state senators, each elected to either a four-year or two-year term. Each senator represents a **district,** or area, of the state. There are 118 members of the house of representatives. Each serves a two-year term and represents a district.

JUDICIAL

The judicial or court system of Illinois has three levels: **circuit courts, appellate courts,** and the **state supreme court.** Judges in all three levels are elected by voters. There are 22 circuit courts in Illinois. Each circuit is an

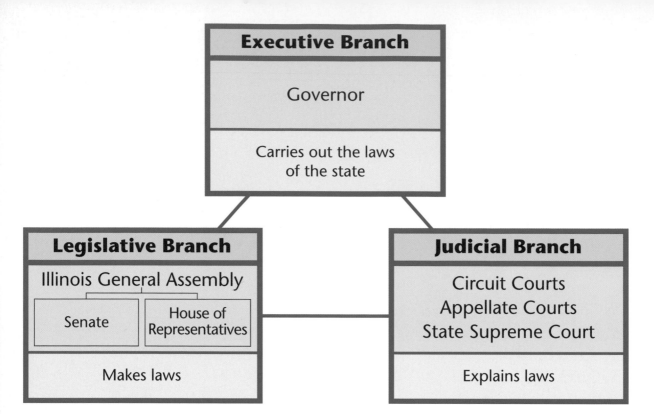

Executive Branch

Governor

Carries out the laws of the state

Legislative Branch

Illinois General Assembly

Senate

House of Representatives

Makes laws

Judicial Branch

Circuit Courts
Appellate Courts
State Supreme Court

Explains laws

The Illinois state government has three branches (above), much like the United States government.

area of the state, similar to a legislative **district. Circuit court** judges serve six-year terms. If a circuit court case is **appealed,** it goes to an **appellate court.** The appellate court hears the case and makes a decision. If the case is again appealed, it finally goes to the **state supreme court.** Appellate court judges and supreme court justices serve ten-year terms. The circuit court of Cook County, Illinois, is the largest in the U.S. It has 404 judges.

ILLINOIS'S CONSTITUTION

Illinois's state constitution was adopted in 1970. A constitution is a written document that states the basic laws and principles by which a state is governed. Illinois had three earlier constitutions. The first was ratified, or approved, in 1818. New constitutions followed in 1848, 1870, and 1970.

The constitution of 1970 made several changes to the way Illinois is governed. It increased the number of state supreme court justices from three to seven. It gave the **governor** greater power to veto any part of a **bill** passed by **lawmakers.** This gave the governor a greater role in deciding how the state spends its money.

The 1970 constitution made it easier for local governments, such as cities and school districts, to manage their own affairs without depending on the state legislature. Finally, the constitution gave added protection to the rights of women and people with disabilities.

Every twenty years, voters are asked if they think Illinois's constitution needs updating. If they think a new constitution is needed, they can vote for a constitutional **convention** to write a new one. Such a convention is made up of **delegates** elected by voters. A constitutional convention has not been called since 1970.

The General Assembly can also propose **amendments,** or changes, to the constitution. Amendments must be approved by three out of five members of each house of the General Assembly. Proposed amendments are then submitted to Illinois voters, who decide whether or not they are accepted.

In Illinois, justices of the state supreme court do not move their residences to the capital. The present Supreme Court Building (below) in Springfield contains small apartments for them.

Capitals and Capitols

The word "capital" refers to a city. The word "capitol" refers to a building. Illinois has had more than one of each of those. When Illinois became a state in 1818, its first capital was Kaskaskia. Kaskaskia was one of Illinois's oldest cities, founded by French settlers in the early 1700s. The first capitol building was a two-story-high brick building. The state paid four dollars per day to rent it.

VANDALIA

In 1820, Vandalia became the second capital of Illinois. It was chosen because it was more centrally located than Kaskaskia and was growing quickly. By the 1830s, some **lawmakers** wanted to move

Vandalia built another new capitol building (below) in 1836. Despite this effort, Illinois lawmakers decided to leave Vandalia for Springfield.

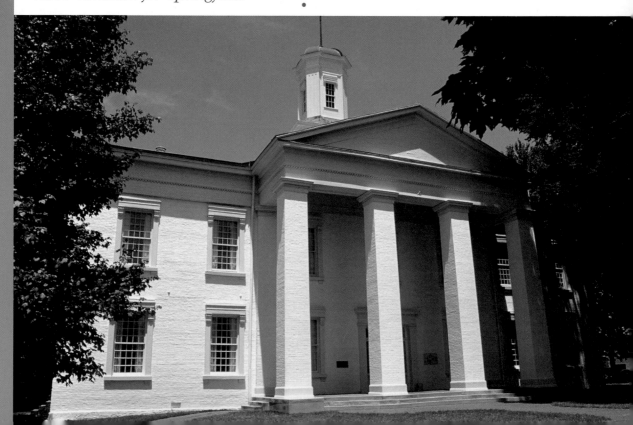

Capitol Statues

Beginning in 1864, the U.S. government invited each state to send statues of important citizens to be displayed in the United States Capitol in Washington, D.C. Illinois is represented by statues of General James Shields (left) and Frances E. Willard (right). Shields was a Civil War general who later became a U.S. senator. Willard founded the Women's Christian Temperance Union, which campaigned to make the sale of alcohol illegal. Willard's statue was the first one of a woman sent by any state.

yet again. They believed Springfield would be a better location because it is even more centrally located. So, in 1839, Springfield became the new state capital.

SPRINGFIELD

The Old State Capitol in Springfield was built between 1837 and 1853. Abraham Lincoln served as a state legislator and gave a famous speech there. In 1858, he referred to the arguments between northern and southern states and said, "A house divided against itself cannot stand."

The Old State Capitol (below) has been preserved as a historic site. The present capitol (right) is also in Springfield.

Construction on the present capitol building in Springfield began in 1868. The first meeting of the General Assembly in that building was held in 1877. Today, the capitol is open to the public. Visitors can watch the General Assembly at work.

Illinois State Symbols

In 1907, Illinois students voted for Illinois's first two state symbols. They selected the violet as the state flower and the oak as the state tree. The General Assembly and the **governor** made their choices official. Since then, schoolchildren have helped select most of the state's symbols.

The violet (above) is Illinois's state flower. About 100 species of violets grow in the U.S. New Jersey, Rhode Island, and Wisconsin have also adopted it as the state flower.

STATE FLOWER: VIOLET

In 1907, Illinois students selected the violet as the state flower. Illinois is home to many different **species,** or kinds, of violets. The dooryard violet is one of the most common of blue violets. Their colorful blooms appear in the spring all across Illinois.

STATE TREE: WHITE OAK

The oak was selected as the state tree in 1907. In 1973, another vote was held among Illinois students to select one species of oak as the official tree. The students selected the white oak. Early settlers moving to Illinois in the 1800s found much of southern Illinois covered with oak trees. They used the strong wood of the white oak to build cabins and make furniture. White oaks often grow as high as 100 feet (30.5 meters). Their wide, spreading branches provide cool shade in the summer. In the fall, their leaves turn red and purple.

White oaks (right) once covered much of southern Illinois. Their strong wood was useful for the settlers building cabins and furniture. The white oak became the official state tree of Illinois in 1973.

STATE BIRD: CARDINAL

Cardinals live throughout Illinois. They are easy to spot. Males are bright red, and females are a mix of brown and red. Cardinals live in Illinois all year long. In winter, their bright color stands out against white snow. They build their nests in bushes, about 5 feet (1.5 meters) off the ground. Cardinals eat insects, fruit, and seeds. Many residents of Illinois place bird feeders in their back yards to attract cardinals. Then they can enjoy the song of the brightly colored bird. The cardinal was selected by a vote of Illinois students. It narrowly defeated the bluebird.

Cardinals (left) are a welcome sight in Illinois winters. The birds were once trapped and sold as songbirds, and their brilliant feathers were used to decorate women's hats. Cardinals are now protected by law.

Fluorite (above) comes in a range of colors. It is a valuable mineral used in the manufacture of aluminum and steel.

STATE MINERAL: FLUORITE

Fluorite is a glass-like **mineral** that comes in colors ranging from deep purple to bright yellow. It often forms beautiful crystals. Fluorite is used in making glass, aluminum, and many chemicals. Illinois was once the largest producer of fluorite in the United States. The General Assembly made fluorite the state mineral in 1965.

STATE INSECT: MONARCH BUTTERFLY

Monarch butterflies live in Illinois from May to October. At summer's end, groups of monarch butterflies begin a 2,000-mile (3,200-kilometer) flight to central Mexico. They spend the winter there. In 1974, a third-grader from Decatur suggested that the monarch butterfly be declared the state insect. The General Assembly made it official in 1975.

Monarch butterflies (right) travel 2,000 miles (3,200 kilometers) each spring to return to Illinois from Mexico. On their way north they lay their eggs on milkweed plants.

STATE FISH: BLUEGILL

Full-grown bluegills weigh less than a pound (0.5 kilograms) and are only about 9 inches (23 centimeters) long. Even though they are small, they are considered one of the best fighting fish in Illinois waters. Bluegills live mostly in small lakes and rivers. They eat insects and smaller fish. The bluegill was selected state fish by a vote of Illinois students in 1986.

The bluegill (above) is small, but an excellent fighter. Bluegills live in small lakes and rivers and grow to be 9 inches (23 centimeters) long.

STATE ANIMAL: WHITE-TAILED DEER

The white-tailed deer is the largest mammal living in Illinois. In the 1800s, hunters drove the white-tailed deer from the state. However, beginning in the 1930s, the white-tailed deer made a comeback in Illinois. Today, white-tailed deer are a common sight in most parts of the state. Illinois schoolchildren selected the white-tailed deer as the state animal in 1980. The white-tailed deer is also the official state animal of eleven other states.

The white-tailed deer (right) has made a comeback in Illinois. It is the largest mammal living in the state and one of the fastest. It can run up to 35 miles (56 kilometers) per hour.

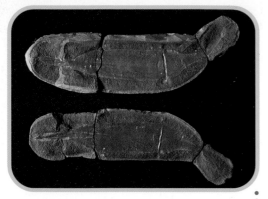

*The Tully Monster (above) swam in Illinois waters 300 million years ago. It fed on shrimp and jellyfish, two **species** that still exist today. Illinois is the only place Tully Monster fossils are found.*

STATE FOSSIL: TULLY MONSTER

The Tully Monster was a soft-bodied animal that swam in the shallow **swamps** that covered Illinois 300 million years ago. **Fossils** are the remains of animals that lived long ago, found in rock or hard earth. The Tully Monster had bendable fins that probably helped make it an excellent swimmer. It also had a long snout ending in a jaw with eight tiny teeth. The Tully Monster probably fed on shrimp, jellyfish, and other small water animals. Tully Monsters are unique to Illinois. Their fossils are found nowhere else in the world. But more than 100 Tully Monster fossils have been found in Illinois. The Tully Monster was named for Francis Tully. He unearthed the first Tully Monster fossils near Braidwood in the 1950s.

Flying the Flag

The state flag of Illinois was designed as part of a contest sponsored by a club called the Daughters of the American Revolution. The winning design, or drawing, was by Lucy Derwent, a member of the club's Rockford chapter. Her design showed part of the state seal set against a white background. In 1970, the state's name was added to the flag. That change was suggested by Bruce McDaniel, who was from Waverly, Illinois. He was then serving in the U.S. Navy. Looking at a display of state flags, he noticed that most other state flags could be easily recognized. However, only people who knew Illinois's state seal could recognize its flag. He suggested that the state's name be added so that the flag could be more easily recognized.

STATE DANCE: SQUARE DANCE

Square dancing is a folk **tradition** brought to the United States by settlers from Europe in the 1600s. Dancers form circles, squares, and other shapes as they dance. Square dancing was made the official state dance in 1990.

STATE PRAIRIE GRASS: BIG BLUESTEM

Big bluestem was one of the grasses that covered much of Illinois before large numbers of settlers moved there in the 1800s. It can grow as high as ten feet (three meters). Its roots extend even deeper into the soil. Its tall, skinny stems turn deep blue late in summer. The Illinois Department of Conservation asked students to select the state prairie grass. In 1989, the General Assembly and Governor James Thompson made big bluestem the state prairie grass.

Square dancing (above) is an American tradition imported from Europe in the 1600s. Square dancers follow the directions of a caller, who calls out different movements and patterns.

Big bluestem (left) can grow as tall as ten feet (three meters). It is the state prairie grass of Illinois. Because of its height, big bluestem can sometimes block the sunlight from other plants, taking over whole areas.

THE GREAT SEAL OF THE STATE OF ILLINOIS

The Great Seal of the State of Illinois is a symbol placed on state documents to show that they are legal and official. The **secretary of state** is the official keeper of the seal. Illinois's seal shows a bald eagle perched on a rock holding a red, white, and blue shield in its **talons.** (The bald eagle also appears on the Great Seal of the United States.) The shield has thirteen stripes and thirteen stars, representing the original thirteen colonies that declared independence from Great Britain. The eagle holds a banner in its beak, which contains the words, "State sovereignty, national union." State sovereignty is the idea that each state has the power to conduct its own business. On the rock are written the dates 1818 and 1868. Illinois became a state in 1818. The current state seal was designed in 1868.

The word "sovereignty" means power over something and freedom from outside control. State sovereignty is what the Confederate states wanted, which is one of the reasons they quit the Union and fought the Civil War (1861–1865). The state seal of Illinois was adopted in 1868, shortly after the Civil War. Because of this, secretary of state Sharon Tyndale changed the design so that "National Union" was more visible, and the word "Sovereignty" was upside-down, making it harder to read.

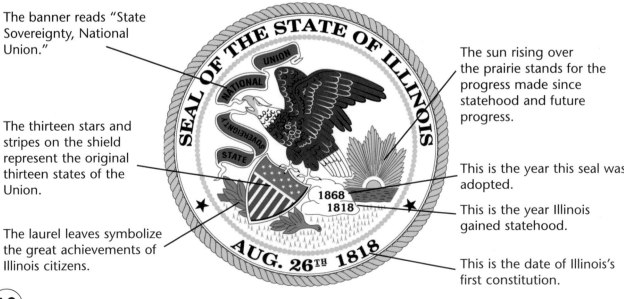

The banner reads "State Sovereignty, National Union."

The thirteen stars and stripes on the shield represent the original thirteen states of the Union.

The laurel leaves symbolize the great achievements of Illinois citizens.

The sun rising over the prairie stands for the progress made since statehood and future progress.

This is the year this seal was adopted.

This is the year Illinois gained statehood.

This is the date of Illinois's first constitution.

STATE SONG: "ILLINOIS"

Lyrics by C.H. Chamberlain
Music by Archibald Johnston

1. By thy rivers gently flowing, Illinois, Illinois, O'er thy prairies verdant growing, Illinois, Illinois, Comes an echo on the breeze, Rustling thro' the leafy trees, And its mellow tones are these, Illinois, Illinois, And it's mellow tones are these, Illinois!

2. From a wilderness of prairies, Illinois, Illinois, Straight thy way and never varies Illinois, Illinois, Til upon the inland sea Stands Chicago, great and free, Turning all the world to thee, Illinois, Illinois, Turning all the world to thee, Illinois!

3. When you heard your country calling, Illinois, Illinois, Where the shot and shell were falling, Illinois, Illinois, When the Southern host withdrew, Pitting Gray against the Blue, There were none more brave than you Illinois, Illinois, There were none more brave than you, Illinois!

4. Not without thy wondrous story, Illinois, Illinois, Can be writ the nation's glory, Illinois, Illinois, On the record of thy years Abra'am Lincoln's name appears, Grant, and Logan, and our tears, Illinois, Illinois, Grant, and Logan,* and our tears, Illinois!

Most people know who Lincoln and Grant are. The Illinois State Song also refers to Logan. John A. Logan was a Union commander during the Civil War (1861–1865). He was later a U.S. senator for Illinois.

19

Land of Lincoln

Abraham Lincoln was born in Kentucky and lived briefly in Indiana. But only Illinois can claim to be the Land of Lincoln. Lincoln moved to Macon County in Illinois in 1830, when he was 21 years old. He lived in Illinois until he became the sixteenth president of the United States in 1861. As a young man, he worked as a store clerk and postmaster in New Salem. He was a member of the Illinois General Assembly from 1834 to 1841. Lincoln also represented Illinois in the United States House of Representatives from 1847 to 1849.

As president, Lincoln led the nation through the Civil War (1861–1865). In 1863, he issued the Emancipation Proclamation, which was the first step in ending slavery in the United States. He was **assassinated** on April 14, 1865. His body was carried back to Illinois from Washington, D.C., on a funeral train. As it slowly crossed the country, thousands of Americans lined the railroad tracks to pay their final respects as the train passed. Lincoln was buried in Springfield's Oak Ridge Cemetery.

The Illinois General Assembly made "Land of Lincoln" the official state slogan in 1955. The state also registered the slogan with the United States Congress, so only Illinois

Lincoln's Springfield home (right) is now a historic site and is open to the public. The Lincoln family lived in the two-story house from 1844 to 1861, when Lincoln became president of the United States.

could use it. The slogan appears on the license plates of Illinois cars.

There are statues and historic sites honoring Abraham Lincoln all over Illinois. It's no wonder Illinois is called the Land of Lincoln. Chicago has two Lincoln statues in its lakefront parks. Charleston is home to the world's largest Lincoln figure, a six-story-high statue. New Salem, where Lincoln lived as a young man, has been preserved as a state historic site. The buildings of that frontier village have been recreated to look as they did in the 1830s.

Springfield is the capital of the Land of Lincoln, so it is fitting that it has more Lincoln sites than any other place. Lincoln's Springfield home has been preserved as a historic site. The Old State Capitol in Springfield was the site of some of Lincoln's most famous speeches. His tomb in Oak Ridge Cemetery attracts many visitors.

*Near Lincoln's tomb is a bronze **bust** of Lincoln (above) by Gutzon Borglum, who also sculpted Mount Rushmore in South Dakota. It has become a tradition for visitors to rub the nose of the Lincoln bust for good luck. So many people have rubbed that nose over the years that it is now shiny.*

Named for Lincoln

There are many cities in the United States named for Abraham Lincoln. But only one city can claim to have been named for Lincoln while he was still living. Lincoln, Illinois, was founded and named in 1853, eight years before Lincoln became president. Lincoln was there for the **dedication** ceremony. Tradition claims he celebrated with a slice of watermelon. Today, a statue of a watermelon slice (left) in downtown Lincoln honors that historic event.

World's Fair

The biggest party Illinois has ever thrown was the 1893 World's Fair in Chicago. The official name of the fair was the World's Columbian Exposition. It was supposed to celebrate the 400th anniversary of Christopher Columbus's voyage to the Americas in 1492. The fair took so long to plan that it opened a year late in 1893.

The fair was held on Chicago's lakefront. More than 27 million people from all over the world attended the fair. Among the most popular exhibits were a 1,500-pound (680-kilogram) statue of Venus de Milo (a copy of a famous statue) made of chocolate, a 70-foot-high (21-meter-high) tower of light bulbs, and an 11-ton (10-metric ton) block of cheese from Canada. The fair introduced many visitors to the wonders of electric power. The fair's electric lights made the buildings glow each night. Most of the buildings constructed for the fair were knocked down after it closed. But the fair's Fine Arts Building is now home to Chicago's Museum of Science and Industry.

BIG WHEEL

The Ferris wheel was first introduced at the World's

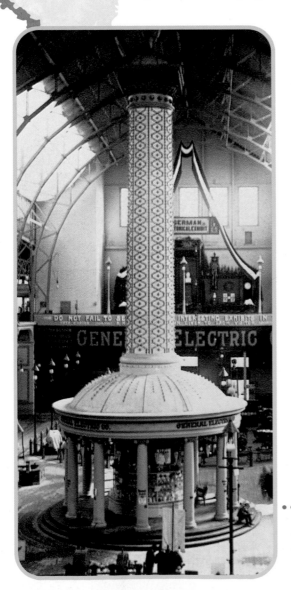

A tower of electric light bulbs (left) was among the attractions at the 1893 World's Columbian Exposition.

State Fairs

Illinois has two state fairs. The DuQuoin State Fair was started in 1923, and is known for its harness races. The harness race (left) is a kind of race between horses pulling light, small carriages. The Illinois State Fair started in 1853. Now held in Springfield, it has been held in twelve different Illinois cities in the past. Visitors enjoy such events as chili-making contests, diaper-decorating contests, and pig races.

Columbian Exposition in 1893. It was named for its inventor, George W. G. Ferris. Ferris was born in Galesburg in 1859. He called his invention the Giant Wheel. The first Ferris wheel was 264 feet (80.5 meters) high. It had 36 boxes, or cars, which could carry up to 60 people each. In all, more than 2,000 passengers could ride the Ferris wheel at one time. On a clear day, riders could see three states. A ride twice around cost 50 cents.

Illinois is still home to famous Ferris wheels. The one at Chicago's Navy Pier is one of the tallest in the world. It stands 150 feet (45.7 meters) high.

Illinois is the home of the first Ferris wheel (above) and a popular one today located on Navy Pier (left) in Chicago.

The First City

The first city in Illinois was built long before Europeans arrived. One thousand years ago, Native Americans lived in a city we call Cahokia. It was located along the Mississippi River, near present-day Collinsville. It was the center of a **culture** that flourished along the Mississippi River. Native Americans lived at Cahokia from 700 to 1400. At its peak, Cahokia may have been home to as many as 15,000 people. That's more people than lived in many European cities during those times.

The people of Cahokia lived in houses arranged in rows, just as in modern cities. They farmed fields of corn, beans, and squash on the edge of the town. They built flat-topped mounds of earth all around the city. Some of these mounds were used as burial locations. On other mounds, important chiefs and priests lived in large houses. The biggest of the mounds at Cahokia is called Monks Mound. It is larger at its base than the Great Pyramid of Egypt.

No one is sure what happened to the people of Cahokia. Wars, disease, or even a loss of trees may have led to the end of their city. By 1400, people no longer lived there. It would be more than 400 years before cities of that size rose again in Illinois.

The ancient city of Cahokia was the center of a culture that lived along the Mississippi River. The people there built earth mounds and houses in rows (below).

The Water Tower

The Great Chicago Fire of 1871 nearly destroyed the city. One of the few buildings to survive the fire was the Chicago Water Tower. The Water Tower was built in 1869 to provide water from Lake Michigan for the city. It rose 154 feet (50 meters) above the city. A two-mile-long tunnel ran from the lake to the tower. The Water Tower was made of blocks of Illinois limestone and was meant to look like a European castle. During the fire, wood buildings all around it burned to the ground, but the Water Tower still stood. To survivors of the fire, the Water Tower became a symbol of the city. Today, the Water Tower is one of Chicago's most popular attractions. It houses a visitor's center and art display.

The Chicago Water Tower (above) is one of the few buildings that survived the fire of 1871.

Collinsville's Water Tower

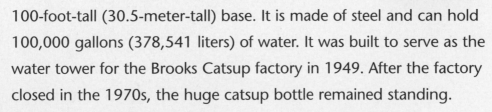

Chicago is not the only city in Illinois with a famous water tower. Collinsville is home to a water tower shaped like a huge catsup bottle (right). The bottle is 70 feet (21.3 meters) tall and sits atop a 100-foot-tall (30.5-meter-tall) base. It is made of steel and can hold 100,000 gallons (378,541 liters) of water. It was built to serve as the water tower for the Brooks Catsup factory in 1949. After the factory closed in the 1970s, the huge catsup bottle remained standing.

Weather

Tornadoes have done some of the worst weather-related damage in Illinois. About 29 tornadoes strike Illinois in a typical year. They can be deadly. In fact, Illinois leads the nation in the number of deaths caused by tornadoes. More than 1,000 Illinoisans have lost their lives to tornadoes since 1916.

Winter storms are common in Illinois. A sudden blizzard caught Illinoisans unprepared in 1837. According to one story, a man riding his horse was surprised by the sudden storm and actually froze in his saddle! A winter storm in 1967 caused $22 million in property damage.

Illinois summers can be dangerous, too. Temperatures can rise to well above 100° Fahrenheit (37.8° Celsius). In 1995, a severe heat wave caused hundreds of deaths in Chicago. Fortunately, such wild weather is the exception, not the rule.

Extreme weather is not uncommon in Illinois. Sudden blizzards (right) can bury the land in snow, and tornadoes can be deadly and destructive (below).

Food

If you like to eat, then Illinois is the place for you. Oak Brook, Illinois, is the home of McDonald's, one of the best-known businesses in the world. The first McDonald's opened in 1955 in Des Plaines, Illinois. It is still standing today, preserved to look the way it did in the 1950s.

Other well-known food producers are based in Illinois. Kraft Foods is famous for its cheese and Miracle Whip dressing. Swift-Ekrich produces bologna and peanut butter. Keebler bakes cookies, and Sara Lee is known for its many desserts. Baby Ruth bars, Milk Duds, Tootsie Rolls, and Jelly Belly candies are all made in Illinois. Twinkies were invented in Illinois in 1930. Americans now eat 500 million Twinkies each year! Illinois also produces chewing gum. In 1892, William Wrigley Jr. first started giving chewing gum away with sales of baking powder. Today, Wrigley's sells about half of the nation's gum.

Taste It Yourself

Chicago is known for some great food, including Chicago-style pizza. Here's a quick recipe for another famous food—the Chicago-style hot dog. You will need:

- 1 all beef hot dog, char-broiled
- 1 poppy seed bun
- 1 heaping teaspoon of mustard
- 1 tablespoon of green relish
- Fresh chopped grilled onions
- 1 large pickle wedge
- 2 slices of ripe plum tomatoes
- A dash of celery salt
- Hot sport peppers, if you'd like

Directions: Place the char broiled hot dog in the bun. Top it with mustard, relish, onions, pickles, and tomatoes. Finish it off with a dash of celery salt. Add the hot sport peppers if you like it hot!

Illinois Stores

Illinois merchants helped develop new ways of selling goods. Aaron Montgomery Ward came up with the idea of letting people shop by mail. In 1872, he started the first mail-order business in the United States, Montgomery Ward & Company of Chicago. The company sent customers a catalog describing goods for sale, such as clothing, tools, and furniture. Customers mailed in their orders, and the company mailed them their purchases. This was popular with people who lived far from cities and could not easily reach stores. The company grew into a worldwide giant during the late 1800s and early 1900s. It went out of business in 2000.

Aaron Montgomery Ward (above) started the first mail-order business in the U.S.

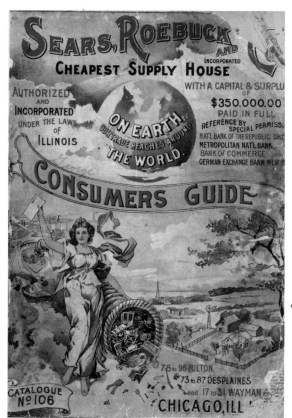

Richard W. Sears and Alvah Roebuck started their own mail-order catalog in 1895. Their company was called Sears, Roebuck and Co., and their first catalog was 532 pages long. Their catalog became known as the place to buy anything. Sears customers could even buy complete parts for a house. Sears, Roebuck and Co. became the world's biggest seller of goods.

This is an early Sears catalog (left) from 1898. The catalog helped people in the country buy things not easily found outside the city. It even offered houses for sale.

The Marshall Field's store in downtown Chicago (left) is a popular meeting place. Marshall Fields was open for business during the Columbian Exposition of 1893. In 1907, the store was expanded to look much as it still does today.

Charles Walgreen (below) opened his first drugstore in Chicago in 1901. Walgreen's drugstores are now found all over the U.S.

In 1881, Marshall Field established the first modern department store in Chicago. He introduced practices such as customer returns, bargain basement sales, and clearly marked pricing. The Marshall Field's store in downtown Chicago is still a popular **landmark.**

Charles C. Walgreen opened his first drugstore in Chicago in 1901. He introduced soda fountains and lunch counters and made drugstores more pleasant places to visit. Today, there are more than 6,000 Walgreen's drugstores.

The Merchandise Mart

When Chicago's Merchandise Mart (left) was built in 1931, it was the largest building in the world. It houses a shopping mall and showrooms for makers of furniture and clothing. It's 25 stories high and covers two city blocks. More than eight miles (thirteen kilometers) of hallways run through the building. It is so big that it has its own zip code! It also has a merchant's hall of fame, honoring great American store-owners.

Architecture and Art

Illinois has some of the world's most famous buildings. It has also been home to some of the most important **architects** in the world. An architect **designs** buildings and oversees their construction. Two of the most important architects of the 1900s lived and worked in Illinois. Frank Lloyd Wright lived in Oak Park, where he designed many houses. Visitors can still tour Wright's home in Oak Park, which he built in 1889. Wright called his architecture "Prairie style," because it was inspired by the Midwestern prairies. He wanted his buildings to blend into the mostly flat Illinois **landscape.** One of his masterpieces is the Dana House in Springfield.

Two examples of Frank Lloyd Wright's work are the Dana-Thomas house in Springfield (left) and Wright's home and studio in Oak Park (below).

In 1938, Mies van der Rohe came to Chicago from Germany. He was in charge of the architecture school at Armour Institute, which is now the Illinois Institute of Technology. He designed a new **campus** for that university. He also designed important glass-and-steel buildings in Chicago and around the world. His Farnsworth House in Plano is one of the **landmarks** of modern architecture.

The first **skyscrapers** were built in Chicago. The Home Insurance Building was the first to have the kind of metal frame that allowed buildings to rise higher than ever. It was completed in 1883. Upon completion in 1891, the sixteen-story-high Monadnock Building in Chicago was the world's tallest. The Sears Tower in Chicago rises 110 stories. It took three years to build and opened in 1973. Chicago's John Hancock Center is 100 stories tall.

The Sears Tower (above) is one of the world's tallest buildings. The building has more than 100 elevators and uses about as much electricity as a town of 35,000 people.

Chicago also has some interesting **sculptures** done by famous artists. One of the most famous sculptures was done by Pablo Picasso. It is located in Daley Plaza in the heart of downtown Chicago.

The Picasso sculpture (left) in downtown Chicago is one of the city's most famous landmarks.

Public Spaces

Chicago has some beautiful lakefront parks. Many of these parks were built as part of a plan made by Daniel Hudson Burnham. Burnham's Plan of Chicago, in 1909, suggested providing open spaces for the enjoyment of the city's rapidly growing population. Today, those parks are popular for both Chicagoans and visitors from all over the world. Each summer, thousands of people attend events like the Chicago Jazz Festival and Taste of Chicago in downtown Grant Park.

For bikers, hikers, skiers, and boaters, Illinois offers more than 60 state parks. They can also visit hundreds of local parks, forest preserves, and **recreation** areas. Boating and fishing are popular on the state's lakes and streams. Two hundred hiking trails crisscross Illinois state parks. The Ozark-Shawnee Trail crosses Shawnee National Forest in southern Illinois. Hikers can also walk the **Trail of Tears** in southern Illinois. Bikers enjoy the rolling landscape of Moraine Hills State Park, near McHenry, in northeast Illinois. Many people visit Pere Marquette State Park, in

Parks line most of Chicago's beautiful lakefront, keeping it open as public space. Grant park (right) hosts many summer events, such as Taste of Chicago. Chicago's lakefront parks were part of Daniel Burnham's plan of 1909.

Illinois State Parks and National Forest

Legend:
- ▲ State Park
- ▢ National Forest

Apple River Canyon, Galena, Lake Le-Aqua-Na, Chain O'Lakes, Rock Cut, Illinois Beach, Waukegan, Moraine Hills, Arlington Heights, Des Plaines, Evanston, Mississippi Palisades, Byron, Rockford, Elgin, Skokie, Oak Park, White Pines Forest, Lowden, Wheaton, Chicago, Morrison-Rockwood, Castle Rock, Aurora, Naperville, Dixon, Illinois & Michigan Canal, Prophetstown, Shabbona Lake, Silver Springs, Joliet, Tampico, Rock Island, Buffalo Rock, Gebhard Woods, Channahon, Moline, Hennepin Canal Parkway, La Salle, Kankakee River, Johnson Sauk Trail, Matthiessen, Illini, William G. Stratton, Kankakee, Bishop Hill, Rock Island Trail, Starved Rock, Kankakee River, Delabar, Galesburg, Jubilee College, Peoria, Eureka, Nauvoo, Pekin, Normal, Argyle Lake, Bloomington, Moraine View, Weinberg-King, Edward R. Madigan, Weldon Springs, Champaign, Kickapoo, Danville, Quincy, Siloam Springs, Sangamon River, Urbana, New Salem, Springfield, Arthur, Walnut Point, Sangchris Lake, Lake Shelbyville, Mattoon, Fox Ridge, Eagle Creek, Wolf Creek, Lincoln Trail, Beaver Dam, Ramsey Lake, Effingham, Père Marquette, Godfrey, Alton, Vandalia, Sam Parr, Embarras River, Horseshoe Lake, Edwardsville, Carlyle Lake, Stephen A. Forbes, Red Hills, East St. Louis, Frank Holten, Eldon Hazlet, South Shore, Cahokia, Centralia, Mt. Vernon, Grayville, Beall Woods, Prairie du Rocher, Wayne Fitzgerrell, Rend Lake, Pyramid, Kaskaskia, Lake Murphysboro, Big Muddy River, Shawneetown, Carbondale, Giant City, Shawnee National Forest, Ferne Clyffe, Dixon Springs, Cave-in-Rock, Fort Massac, Cairo, Fort Defiance, Ohio River, Mississippi River, Illinois River, Rock River, Fox River

There are state parks in every region of Illinois. The Shawnee National Forest, in southern Illinois, is the only national forest in the state.

western Illinois, to see bald eagles and enjoy wonderful views of the Mississippi River.

The Chicago River

The Chicago River used to flow into Lake Michigan. In 1900, **engineers** changed its direction, to keep pollution out of Chicago's water supply. Now it flows south, toward the Illinois and Mississippi Rivers. Chicago also has 45 movable bridges, to let tall ships pass under. That's more than any other city in the world.

Museums and More

Illinois's museums include Adler Planetarium and Astronomy Museum, Art Institute, Chicago Historical Society, DuSable Museum of African American History, The Field Museum of Natural History, Illinois State Museum, and the Museum of Science and Industry. All of these museums are located in Chicago, except Illinois State Museum, which is in Springfield.

For animal lovers, the Chicago area offers two zoos and The Shedd Aquarium. The Lincoln Park Zoo was established in 1868. It is the nation's oldest, free public zoo. The Brookfield Zoo is just west of downtown Chicago in Brookfield, Illinois. The Shedd Aquarium offers a chance to see beluga whales and pacific white-sided dolphins swimming in nearly 3 million gallons (11,356,235 liters) of saltwater.

Chicago's Art Institute (below) was built in 1893 for the Columbian Exposition. The museum houses more than 300,000 works of art.

Writers

Illinois has produced some of the nation's most important writers. L. Frank Baum moved to Chicago from his native New York. Later, he wrote *The Wonderful Wizard of Oz*, and other books for young readers. Edgar Rice Burroughs was born in Chicago in 1875. He worked as a cowboy, soldier, salesman, and at other jobs before he began writing fantasy stories. His most famous book was *Tarzan the Ape Man,* completed in May 1912.

Ernest Hemingway was born in Oak Park in 1899. He drove an ambulance in World War I and later lived in Europe. He wrote about both experiences in his books and stories. In 1952, he won a **Pulitzer Prize** for his book *The Old Man and the Sea*. Two years later, he won the **Nobel Prize** for **literature.**

Edgar Lee Masters's *Spoon River Anthology* is one of America's best-known books of poetry. Masters lived most of his life in Lewistown. Carl Sandburg was the son of a Galesburg **blacksmith.** He became one of the world's best-known poets. One of his most famous poems, "Chicago," described work in the city's factories and **stockyards.** It gave Chicago the nickname "Hog Butcher for the World." Gwendolyn Brooks wrote poems about the lives of African Americans in large cities like Chicago. In 1950, she won a Pulitzer Prize. In 1969, she was named **poet laureate** of Illinois.

L. Frank Baum wrote for Chicago newspapers before writing The Wonderful Wizard of Oz *(below).*

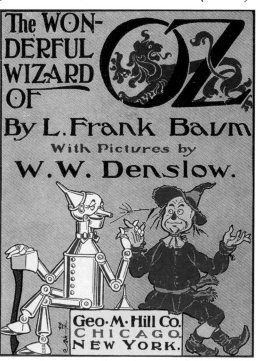

The WONDERFUL WIZARD OF Oz
By L. Frank Baum
With Pictures by
W. W. Denslow.

Geo. M. Hill Co.
CHICAGO.
NEW YORK.

Music

Jazz music was part of the African-American **culture** of New Orleans, Louisiana, in the late 1800s. In the early 1900s, many African Americans from the south moved north to Illinois in what is called The Great Migration. They came looking for jobs in factories, but they brought jazz music with them. Illinois became a popular place for jazz musicians and audiences. Chicago alone was home to hundreds of jazz clubs.

Louis Armstrong (above) also performed in films and helped make jazz popular around the world.

Louis Armstrong was part of the wave of African Americans who headed north to Illinois. He was born in New Orleans in 1898, and learned to play trumpet there. In 1922, he moved to Chicago. His trumpet playing and singing made him one of the biggest stars in jazz.

Benny Goodman was born in Chicago in 1909. He was white, but his orchestras featured many of the top

Illinois Orchestra

Illinois has long been home to great classical music. Belleville's symphony orchestra is the second oldest in the nation. It was founded in 1867. The Chicago Symphony Orchestra was founded in 1891, and quickly became one of the world's greatest orchestras.

African-American musicians of the 1930s and 1940s. He was one of the first bandleaders to start bands with both white and African-American musicians. His clarinet playing earned him the nickname "King of Swing."

Miles Davis was born in Alton in 1926. He helped pioneer the "cool jazz" sound of the late 1940s. In the 1960s, he became one of the first jazz musicians to use electronic instruments.

Miles Davis (below) introduced new styles to jazz. His music and styles varied greatly from one period of his life to the next.

Chicago has long been an important source of blues music and musicians. Many of the world's great blues musicians perform at the Chicago Blues Festival each summer. Chicago musicians even produced their own brand of blues music, called Chicago soul. Chicago soul often featured several lead singers and the use of an **artificially** high voice called falsetto.

Sports

Illinois has no shortage of professional sports teams and stars. It has a long, proud history of great teams and fans.

JORDAN AND THE BULLS

Statues are usually reserved for presidents or generals. But one of the best-loved statues in Chicago honors an athlete. It is the statue of Michael Jordan outside the United Center. The United Center is the home of the Chicago Bulls basketball team. Jordan played for the Bulls from 1984 to 1993, and from 1996 to 1998. During that time, he led the Bulls to six National Basketball Association (NBA) championships. Many people consider Jordan the greatest basketball player of all time. He led the NBA in scoring ten times. He also played for U.S. Olympic basketball teams that won gold medals in 1984,

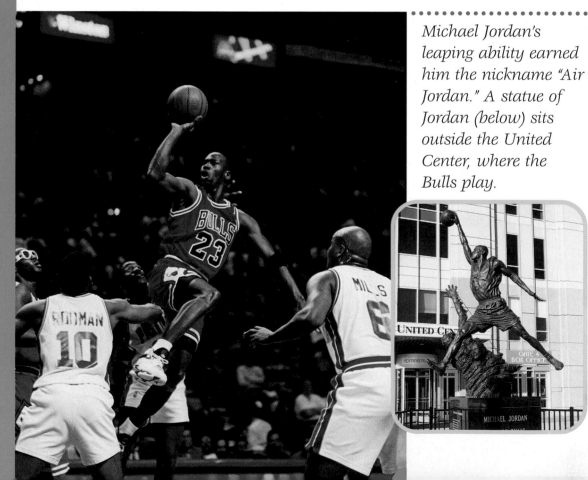

Michael Jordan's leaping ability earned him the nickname "Air Jordan." A statue of Jordan (below) sits outside the United Center, where the Bulls play.

Bat Column

You can't hit a home run with it, but this baseball bat is still a favorite of Chicagoans. Bat Column (right) is a **sculpture** by Claes Oldenburg, completed in 1976. It stands in downtown Chicago, and is more than 100 feet (30.5 meters) tall.

1992, and 1996. His accomplishments made him one of the world's best-known athletes.

Jordan also sought out challenges away from the basketball court. He played baseball for a minor league team of the Chicago White Sox in 1994. In 2000, he became part owner of the NBA's Washington Wizards. However, Jordan could not stop playing basketball for long. In 2001, he came out of retirement once more to play for the Wizards.

CUBS, WHITE SOX, AND BLACK SOX

Chicago was one of the first cities to have a professional baseball team. The team that eventually became the

Sammy Sosa and the Cubs (right) play in historic Wrigley Field (below). Wrigley Field was built in 1914 and is the second-oldest ballpark in the nation. The Cubs began playing in 1871, but weren't called the Cubs until 1902.

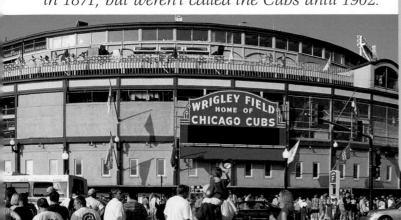

The White Sox (right) defeated Cleveland in the first official American League game on April 22, 1901. The White Sox defeated the Cubs the only time the two teams met in the World Series in 1906.

The new Comiskey Park (left) opened on April 18, 1991, across the street from the old Comiskey Park. The new park had 40,000 seats. A record 2,934,154 fans came to the stadium its first year.

Chicago Cubs began playing in 1871—the same year as the Great Chicago Fire. In fact, the fire destroyed the team's home field.

The Chicago White Sox started playing in 1900. They were among the first members of the American League. The White Sox and the Cubs have met in only one World

Baseball in Skirts?

The All-Girls Professional Baseball League was founded in 1943, by P.K. Wrigley, the owner of the Chicago Cubs. Wrigley wanted the league's players "to look like women and play like men." Their uniforms included short skirts. The league had four teams in Illinois—the Rockford Peaches, the Springfield Sallies, the Peoria Redwings, and the Chicago Colleens. The league ended in 1954. It was the subject of a movie called *A League of Their Own*.

All-Star Game

Baseball's first major-league All-Star Game was played in Chicago's Comiskey Park (left) in 1933. The American League beat the National League, 4-2. Babe Ruth of the New York Yankees hit the game-winning home run. Over 49,000 people witnessed baseball history that day.

Series. In 1906, the Chicago Cubs had the best record in all of baseball. However, the **underdog** White Sox defeated them in the World Series.

The last Cubs world championship was in 1908. The last time the White Sox won was in 1917. In 1919, the White Sox lost to the Cincinnati Reds in the World Series. Eight White Sox players were later accused of planning with **gamblers** to lose the World Series on purpose. When their plan was revealed after the World Series, the players were banned from baseball forever. The 1919 team became known as the Black Sox.

The White Sox and the Cubs are not the only professional baseball teams to call Illinois home. Minor-league teams play in cities such as Peoria, Rockford, Schaumburg, and Geneva.

BEAR DOWN, CHICAGO BEARS

In 1920, a young athlete named George Halas helped start the first major professional football league. It was called the American Professional Football Association. It included three teams from Illinois—the Rock Island Independents, Chicago Racine Cardinals, and Decatur Staleys.

The 1985 Chicago Bears team (right) was a popular and successful one. They only lost one game in their regular season and went on to become the Superbowl champions.

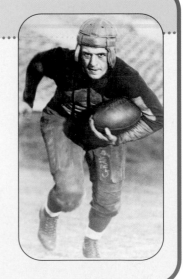

The Chicago Bears play in Soldier Field (left), which was remodeled beginning in 2002. Soldier Field was built in the 1920s and was meant to look like an ancient Greek or Roman stadium.

Halas coached and played for the Staleys. The team was sponsored by the A.E. Staley Company of Decatur, makers of corn syrup. In 1922, the company gave Halas control of the team. He moved it to Chicago and changed its name to the Bears. That same year, the league changed its name to the National Football League (NFL).

The Bears became one of the league's best teams. Halas coached them to eight NFL championships. They became

The Galloping Ghost

Professional football's first big star was Harold "Red" Grange (right). He was a star running back first at Wheaton High School, then at the University of Illinois. His exciting runs earned him the nickname "The Galloping Ghost." In 1925, he turned professional and began playing for the Chicago Bears. The Bears went on a national tour that made Grange a national star and helped make professional football popular.

known as the "Monsters of the Midway." (The Midway was the section of parkland built for the 1893 World's Fair in Chicago.) The 1985 Chicago Bears rank as one of the best teams in NFL history. They were led by Coach Mike Ditka, who had played for the Bears under George Halas.

There are other popular sports in Illinois. The Chicago Blackhawks play professional ice hockey in the National Hockey League (NHL). The Chicago Fire is a professional soccer team with many faithful fans.

Women's soccer received a lot of attention in Chicago in 1999. The U.S. women's soccer team won the World Cup that year. One of the games, against Nigeria, was played at Soldier Field in Chicago. The women of Team U.S.A. won 7-1. A record crowd of 65,080 people attended the game.

The U.S. women's soccer team defeated Nigeria in this World Cup game (below), played at Soldier Field in 1999. That U.S. team made women's soccer very popular in the United States.

Very Unique

I t would be impossible to include all of the interesting things that make Illinois unique. Here's one last sampling of some fun facts.

HOW TALL?

Robert P. Wadlow of Alton, Illinois, was the tallest person in history, according to the **Guinness Book of World Records.** He stood 8 feet, 11 inches (2.7 meters) tall and weighed 490 pounds (222 kilograms). By the time he was eight years old, Wadlow already stood 6 feet, 2 inches (1.9 meters) tall! In 1985, Alton put up a statue to honor him.

Chicago's First United Methodist Church claims to be the tallest church in the world. Housed in a Chicago skyscraper, its steeple is 568 feet (173 meters) tall.

Wadlow's mother, father, brothers, and sisters (above) were all of ordinary size, but young Robert grew very quickly.

FIRE PREVENTION

National Fire Prevention Week is held every year in October. President Calvin Coolidge proclaimed the first one in 1925. It is held in October in memory of the Great Chicago Fire, which began on October 9, 1871.

Chicago's First United Methodist Church is located in downtown Chicago. Its "Chapel in the Sky" has a beautiful view of the city.

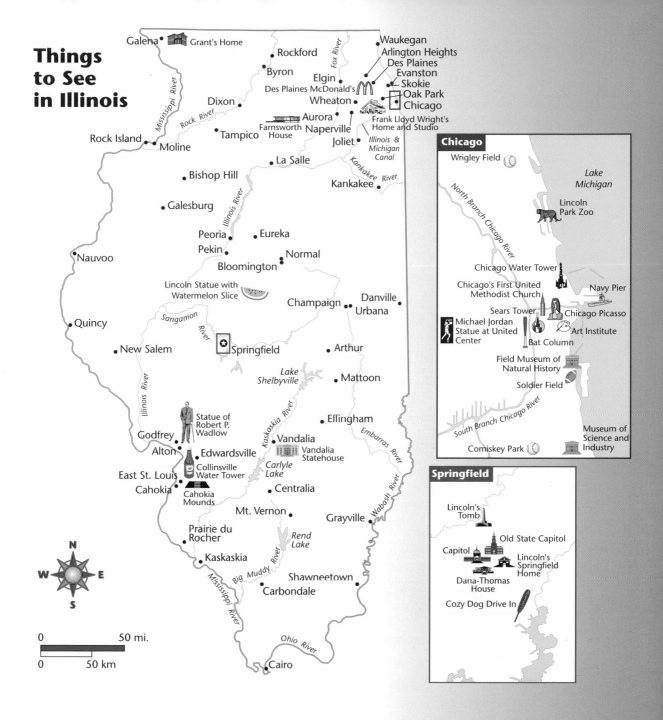

Things to See in Illinois

Galena • Grant's Home
Rockford
Byron
Dixon
Elgin
Des Plaines McDonald's
Wheaton
Aurora
Farnsworth House
Naperville
Joliet
Illinois & Michigan Canal
Rock Island
Moline
La Salle
Bishop Hill
Galesburg
Peoria
Pekin
Bloomington
Lincoln Statue with Watermelon Slice
Champaign
Danville
Urbana
Quincy
New Salem
Springfield
Arthur
Lake Shelbyville
Mattoon
Statue of Robert P. Wadlow
Godfrey
Alton
Edwardsville
Vandalia
Vandalia Statehouse
Collinsville Water Tower
Carlyle Lake
East St. Louis
Cahokia
Cahokia Mounds
Centralia
Mt. Vernon
Grayville
Prairie du Rocher
Rend Lake
Kaskaskia
Shawneetown
Carbondale
Cairo

Waukegan
Arlington Heights
Des Plaines
Evanston
Skokie
Oak Park
Chicago
Frank Lloyd Wright's Home and Studio

Tampico
Nauvoo
Eureka
Normal
Effingham
Kankakee

Rivers: Mississippi River, Rock River, Fox River, Illinois River, Kankakee River, Sangamon River, Kaskaskia River, Embarras River, Wabash River, Big Muddy River, Ohio River

N W E S

0 — 50 mi.
0 — 50 km

Chicago

Wrigley Field
North Branch Chicago River
Lincoln Park Zoo
Lake Michigan
Chicago Water Tower
Chicago's First United Methodist Church
Navy Pier
Sears Tower
Chicago Picasso
Michael Jordan Statue at United Center
Art Institute
Bat Column
Field Museum of Natural History
Soldier Field
South Branch Chicago River
Comiskey Park
Museum of Science and Industry

Springfield

Lincoln's Tomb
Old State Capitol
Capitol
Lincoln's Springfield Home
Dana-Thomas House
Cozy Dog Drive In

CORN DOGS

Illinois is the land of corn, so it's no wonder that it's also the birthplace of the corn dog. What's a corn dog? Take a hot dog, dip it in corn meal, and deep fry it, and you have a corn dog. Corn dogs were introduced to the world in 1949, at the Cozy Dog Drive In in Springfield.

The first corn dog was actually called a "cozy dog."

Glossary

amendment change in, or addition to, a bill or law, such as an amendment to a constitution

appeal bring a case before a higher court for review of the decision of a lower court

appellate court court that hears cases that have already been tried in a lower court and reviews the judgment of that lower court

architect person who designs buildings and gives advice on their construction

artificial not real; put on just for an effect

assassinate murder a leader for political reasons or for pay

attorney general chief law officer of a state or nation

bill proposed law to be considered for approval by lawmakers

blacksmith person who makes iron objects by heating them and hammering them on an anvil. Blacksmiths often make horseshoes.

budget plan for spending a certain amount of money in a certain amount of time

bust sculpture of the head and shoulders of a person

campus land around a college

chariot two-wheeled vehicle pulled by a horse and used in ancient times

circuit court court that sits in two or more places in one judicial district; a legal case is first heard in a circuit court

comptroller public official who keeps track of the money a government spends

convention formal meeting of people for a common purpose

culture ideas, skills, arts, and way of life of a certain people at a certain time

dedication ceremony for naming or establishing a building or monument

delegate person sent to a meeting to represent a community

design plan a thing to be built

district part of a state, city, or country

engineer person who designs machines or large public works

executive branch branch of government that makes sure the laws of a state or nation are carried out

fossil remains or traces of a living thing of long ago

gamble take part in a game in which the players make bets; a gambler is someone who takes part in such a game

governor person elected to be the head of a state of the United States; the governor is the head of the executive branch of a state government

invest put money to use in the hopes of making a profit

judicial branch branch of government that includes the courts; the judicial branch explains or interprets the laws of the state or nation

landmark important place or building that people recognize

lawmaker person who makes laws

legislation laws

legislative branch branch of government that makes laws

legislature governmental body that makes and changes laws

lieutenant governor second-in-command of a state, after the governor

literature writing of lasting value

mineral solid substance formed in the earth by nature and obtained by mining

Nobel Prize one of several prizes awarded each year for achievements in various fields

poet laureate poet honored for excellence by a state or nation

Pulitzer Prize one of a group of prizes awarded each year for works of journalism, history, and biography

recreation exercise or other forms of enjoyable activity

sculpture kind of work of art produced by carving or shaping a hard material; a sculptor is a person who creates such art

secretary of state public official responsible for keeping state records and the state seal

skyscraper very tall building

species group of living things that resemble one another, have common ancestors, and can breed with one another

state supreme court highest court in the state, which decides cases that have been through the circuit and appellate courts

stockyard place where hogs, cattle, and other animals are kept

swamp wet, low-lying area with trees growing in shallow water

talon claw of a bird

tomb burial place for the dead

tornado column of air that is very fast, shaped like a funnel, and usually quite destructive

tradition custom or belief that is handed down from generation to generation

Trail of Tears trail the Cherokee people followed when the U.S. government forced them to move from their land in the southeast to a reservation in Oklahoma. Many Cherokee people died on the difficult journey, which is why the trail became known as the "Trail of Tears."

treasurer person in charge of the money of a government

underdog person, team, or side that is expected to lose a contest of some kind

veto right of a chief executive, such as a governor or president, to reject a law passed by lawmakers

More Books to Read

Bruun, Erik. *Illinois State Shapes.* New York: Black Dog and Leventhal Publishing, 2001.

Marsh, Carole. *Illinois Jeopardy.* Peachtree City, Ga.: Gallopade International, 2000.

Marsh, Carole. *Illinois Timeline: A Chronology of Illinois History, Mystery, Trivia, Legend, Lore and More.* Peachtree City, Ga.: Gallopade International, 1995.

McAuliffe, Emily. *Illinois Facts and Symbols.* Minnetonka, Minn.: Capstone Press, 1998.

Thompson, Kathleen. *Illinois.* New York: Raintree Steck-Vaughn, 1996.

Index

About the Author

Andrew Santella lives in Trout Valley, Illinois, and is a lifelong resident of the state of Illinois. He is the author of 25 nonfiction books for children. He also writes for publications such as *GQ* and the *New York Times Book Review*.